WAS IT A DREAM?

Navigating Life's Journey Through Poetry

BOOK 1

LARADA HORNER-MILLER

HORNER PUBLISHING COMPANY

PRAISE FOR LARADA HORNER-MILLER

The poems in Larada's book pull you into her life and expose her sorrow. The nature poem is realistic. You can feel the sticks with the loose bark between your fingers and smell the mingled forest smells. I didn't want to finish and suddenly I was done! She is a natural and honest poet.

~Sherrie L. Crandal,, MEd

Larada Horner-Miller has invited you to join her on a very personal reminiscing of parts of her life. I found it to be evocative and emotion filled. Her descriptions take you to the time and place where she was, and I found myself identifying with parallels in my own life. It's the best poetry I've read in a long time and think you'll be similarly taken with her works. I recommend it highly and thank her for sharing it with us all.

~John Parus
Elite Reader at <u>AuthorsXP.com</u> and both an ARC and Beta for multiple authors. You can find my reviews on Amazon, Goodreads, BookBub, and other places.

Larada's poetry emerges as reflective, and thought-provoking. She captures words, and images profoundly, and turns them into transformational philosophies that combine conscious, compassionate alignment in different worlds, different phases. Her life is shown in segments. The world around her is shown in segments. The main idea of the book is struggles, obstacles, and coming to terms with decisions made or not made. My favourite parts are where she describes nature. Her poetry shines through making her a "life-traveller." The book motivates readers to look at life's ups, and downs in a creative way.

~Michelle Kafka
Freelance writer and poet. Her work has appeared in print, and online. Published in Chrysanthemum Poetry Magazine Spring Issue, Bottle Rockets Poetry Journal Summer Issue, Hello Horror Literary Journal Winter Issue 13, and Haiku and Micro-poetry International. Ms. Kafka has been writing for over twenty years.

Horner-Miller's poetry dances between memory and moment, weaving a tapestry of life that is both deeply personal and universally resonant. 'Was It a Dream?' is a testament to the enduring power of the poetic voice.

~Autumn Williams, Author of *Clouds on the Ground*

Copyright © 2024 by Larada Horner-Miller All rights reserved.

To buy books in quantity for corporate use or incentives, call (505) 323-798 or e-mail larada@LaradasBooks.com

ISBN-13: 979-8-9896886-1-6 (Horner Publishing Company)

No part of this book may be reproduced in any form or by any electronic or mechanical means, including information storage and retrieval systems, without written permission from the author, except for the use of brief quotations in a book review.

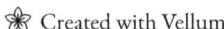 Created with Vellum

CONTENTS

Introduction	xi
1. 1980s & 90s	1
Visiting a Poem Thirty-Eight Later	3
A Modern-Day Pilgrimage to Chimayó	9
My Love Poem to Mike,	17
Dad	21
High Heels	23
Sails Dance	25
Slender Lips	27
Years & Silence	29
A Part of Me Died	31
A New Mexico Desert Breeze	33
2. Rio Grande Writing Project, 1995	37
Forty Makes a Difference	39
Childless	41
My Bracelet	45
Along the Way, Nature Screams at Me!	47
3. 1995-1996 Writing With My Students	55
Playing with Words	57
If The World Could Hold Us!	59
If The World Could Hold Us!	61
It Can All Be All Right	63
4. 1996 My Dad	67
My Humor	69
A Storyteller Forever	71
5. 1997	77
Was It a Dream?	79
6. 1998	85
Canada	87

Lake Coeur D'Alene, Idaho	91
A Laundromat	93
My Heart Was Strangled	95
He Wanted to Touch Her	97
A Child's First Steps	99
Conclusion	101
About the Author	103
Also by Larada Horner-Miller	105
Future Projects & Would You. . .?	107
AND NOW, WOULD YOU. . .?	109
Excerpt from Book #2 of Navigating Life's Journey Through Poetry Series	111
Notes	113

DEDICATION

- To my husband, Lin, for helping me identify myself as a poet and being willing to read this book even though he doesn't like poetry
- To all my readers of my previous books who have enjoyed my poetry peppered here and there

Grab a free chapbook featuring my poetry from two poetry classes I took in 2002 and 2003 to sample more of my poetry here: subscribepage.io/VTpxUU

"Poetry is language at its most distilled and most powerful."

~Rita Dove

INTRODUCTION

"Instructions for living a life:
   Pay attention.
   Be astonished.
   Tell about it."

~Mary Oliver, "Sometimes"*

"A poet?" I questioned.

---

* Mary Oliver, *Devotions*, (Penguin Press, 2017), 105.

"Yes, you're a poet!" Lin, my husband, responded enthusiastically.

While lounging in our hot tub one beautiful New Mexico evening last year, Lin asked me what word I'd use to describe myself in my writing. I mulled it over in my mind. Did he mean genre? Author? Writer? I don't even remember what I said, but his answer floored me—"Poet!"

I thought, four of my seven published books feature my poetry. I've written a lot of poems, but I'm not Shakespeare or Milton. I don't rhyme and have meter in my poetry. Could I be a poet?

Even though it was something so familiar and deep-seated in me that came to light, I had needed someone else to identify it, to identify who I really was—a poet!

After this refreshing discovery, I ran to our storage shed to find all my old poems. I knew exactly where my journals were. I made a beeline to the box, and there they were! After dusting them off, I marveled at the work I hadn't looked at in years, in decades. That joyous revelation—that I was not just a writer but also a poet—changed my life as an author.

As I mused over Mary Oliver's poetic "Instructions for living a life," I realized that, yes, I have "paid attention" by retelling my life's journey through poetry for years, yet really didn't realize it until I put this poetry series together. This first book begins with a solitary poem written in 1986 that starts with a trip to the Mayan Indian ruin in Cobá, Mexico and ends with me in Spokane, Washington doing laundry in a laundromat, "paying attention" to a child's first steps.

While that first poem focuses on a travel adventure, this whole book will take you on a journey through my life in the 80s and 90s, when I was in my late thirties and early forties, an unsettled time in my life. I reveal a variety of my vulnerable "heart hurts," like being childless at forty. That was monumental for me, a big piece of my pain.

Looking back at these poems, I am astonished at how deeply vulnerable I am. When I wrote these poems, it was to process my life at that specific moment, not to share my innermost thoughts with the world.

Because of that, there are so many different key elements throughout: the pain, the celebration, the wonder, the astonishment, as Mary Oliver says. So, if you're looking for a central theme, my collection may upset you because I share a hodgepodge of life events, but it is my story.

My first wedding was September 9, 1973, and at that point in my life, I did not see myself as a writer much less a poet. I wrote nothing—poetry or prose. I was still in pain from some past traumas, so I couldn't see the trees for the forest.

Because of that, I struggled through that relationship, and we ended up divorcing in 1980. For eight years, I actively struggled with alcoholism. That sounds like a short span of time, but for women, the average length of their drinking years is seven years, so I was right there. During those years, I didn't write any poetry.

From 1982 to 1986, I attended Colorado State University —forty years ago! After a false start for my freshman year in Occupational Therapy, I switched my major to English with a teaching concentration two weeks into the semester and walked into a class with the professor reading Beowulf in Old English. It felt like a foreign language, but I persevered. I was twenty-eight years old when I went to the university for the first time, so I had forgotten anything I had learned in high school, not that I had a very strong background in literature to begin with.

At the beginning of that first semester, I remember sitting in an English literature class and the professor asked a probing question about sirens. Having no clue how a siren connected to the reading, I sat with my hand firmly not raised, but because of my good-student-mindset, I almost responded anyway. When a student spouted off the answer sought for, my mouth dropped! My only reference to a siren was a noisy alarm on emergency equipment. Sirens on the rocks, warning sailors. I had no idea, and apparently, I hadn't studied the passage for the class that day enough.

From then on, I knuckled down and prepared for each class thoroughly, realizing I almost had an embarrassing moment in front of my peers ten years younger than me.

It was in those English and American literature classes that I found poetry. I stumbled through the poetry sections of my classes, in awe of the meaning the professors gleaned from the words lined up in stanzas.

In my upper-level classes, I eagerly absorbed the Shakespeare and Milton tomes and internalized their influence, unknowingly preparing to embrace my own inner poet years later.

There at the university, I started writing for my education classes and realized through good grades and positive comments made by different professors that I certainly did have the ability to write an educational paper. Though I never thought I'd be publishing not only one, but four poetry books in this series, and more.

In 1986, I graduated in the top four percent of my class with a B.A. in Education, a minor in Spanish, and concentration in Education.

I got sober on December 22, 1988. I've often thought that my poetry writing paralleled my recovery, but it was in 1986 that I wrote that first poem about Cobá, which I find so rich. Writing that poem and graduating ignited something in me that year, and that was the first glimmer I had that I was a poet.

I can see now that already I was starting to see myself as a poet and noting life.

Four of my seven published books feature poetry and prose, so it's not a new genre for me. While teaching middle school language arts and literature, I taught a poetry unit every year, but I didn't take myself seriously as a poet. I was a middle school teacher. I only dabbled in poetry.

I also participated as a fellow in the Rio Grande Writing Project, an affiliate of the National Writing Project, a professional development program for teachers. It promoted writing "across the curriculum"—in math, social studies, science, and electives, as well as language arts and literature classes.

During this time, I followed the training of Nancy Atwell's book, *In the Middle*, where I learned about "Writing and Reading Workshop," her successful plan for teaching writing and reading to middle school students. This book changed my classroom. I wrote daily with my students at the beginning of class. I would write a prompt on the board before class so the students knew to sit down, open their writing notebooks, copy the prompt, and respond. Each day, I timed it for seven minutes. When I finished my daily teacher chores, like attendance, I grabbed my writing journal and a chair near a student and wrote. I wanted them to see me as a writer and often I chose poetry to express myself.

By focusing on the writing process, I grounded this writing time in Natalie Goldberg's book, *Writing Down the Bones*, and introduced my students to her preferred writing practice, a timed free write. She listed seven things to consider for this time:

1. Keep your hand moving. No matter what, don't stop . . .
2. Don't cross out.
3. Don't worry about spelling, punctuation, or grammar.
4. Lose control. Let it rip . . .

5. Don't think. Don't get logical.
6. Go for the jugular.[*]
7. You are free to write the worst junk in the world [†] (I added, "in the universe!")

Can you imagine a writing teacher telling her students not to worry about spelling, punctuation, or grammar? My students loved it, and their writing blossomed. Then when the poetry unit came up, I guided them through haikus, free verse, and self-expression. It became a favorite of theirs and mine.

Yet at this time, it was a nominal gesture! I didn't feel like a writer, much less a poet. That identity came years later.

Then something happened! Poetry became the genre I ran to when life tilted in ways I had no control over, good or bad—my mom's death, the coronavirus pandemic, life!

Almost forty years after writing my first poem, I gathered all my poems together and realized I had written enough poetry to fill at least four poetry books. After taking Natalie Goldberg's writing practice class during the pandemic and reading her book, *Three Simple Lines: A Writer's Pilgrimage into the Heart and Homeland of Haiku*, I've currently moved to haikus to express my life, yet I still write free verse occasionally.

Today I write poetry when I'm happy; I write poetry when I'm sad. I write about what's important and about what's trivial.

This collection of poetry, spanning the first fifteen years of my poetry writing, takes a peek into me and my world. From the luscious green jungles of Mexico to the beautiful purple orange sunsets of New Mexico. From losing my dad and my

---

[*] Natalie Goldberg, *Writing Down the Bones* (Shambhala Publications, Inc., 1986), 8.
[†] Natalie Goldberg, *Wild Mind: Living The Writer's Life* (Bantam New Age Book., 1990), 4.

second and third husbands to living a life without my own child.

Today, several famous poets influence me: contemporaries Mary Oliver and Billy Collins, classics William Shakespeare and Emily Dickinson, and Native Americans Joy Harjo and Louise Erdrich.

Some of those influences are evident in my poems. Magical realism from my Spanish literature classes seeped into my poem on Cobá, for instance. George Strait, my country and western hero, shows up in the title poem ("Was it a Dream?"), doing what I love to do besides write—dance! His advice became my motto for life.

But it was when I found Mary Oliver's "Instructions for living a life" in her poem, "Sometimes" that I realized I had followed her directions in my poetry to the tee. She was an influence without my even knowing!

So please, step into my world of poetry and walk through my journey with me in this first book as I look at personal growth, reflection, and the twists and turns life can make.

Chapter One
1980S & 90S

As a poet in the late 80s and living in Raton, New Mexico after college, I only wrote two poems. I hadn't yet embraced myself as a poet and didn't see poems all around me.

But when I moved to Albuquerque in 1991 and participated in the Rio Grande Writing Project in 1992, my poetry exploded. I began seeing poetry everywhere.

I include here a poem I wrote for my second husband and read at our wedding. Sadly, we divorced.

In 1993, Jeanne Greenhouse, Eleanor Schick, and Carol Kreis, who I learned from in the Rio Grande Writing Project, honored me by asking me to join the staff as a teacher for the workshop that summer. Afterwards, I attended two advanced workshops in 1994 and 1995.

One fun-filled activity we did while attending the Writing Project was a Drive-By Poetry Reading on Central Avenue across from the University of New Mexico—a very busy intersection. We stood on the street corner in front of the Frontier

Restaurant and read poetry to anyone who walked (drove) by! We shocked students, professors, everyone!

I saw poetry everywhere!

VISITING A POEM THIRTY-EIGHT LATER

Thirty-eight years ago, I wrote this poem after my memorable adventure in Cobá, Mexico in the summer of 1985. Laying solemnly unattended on my computer, it haunted me for many years because of my surreal experience there.

After studying the genre of magical realism at Colorado State University with my Spanish literature teachers, it fascinated me—reality with a dash of magic.

So, what is magical realism:

"Within a work of magical realism, the world is still grounded in the real world, but fantastical elements are considered normal in this world. Like fairy tales, magical realism novels and short stories blur the line between fantasy and reality."*

---

* https://www.masterclass.com/articles/what-is-magical-realism#what-is-magical-realism

Look Closely—I am standing on the middle of Coba, Mexico

Cobá—I Was There!!

> Written - March, 1986
> Revised – July 25, 2021

The year was 1985.

Walking down an overgrown jungle path
   with my friend Lynn,
      an iguana crosses my trail—
      toucan birds grunt and croak

above my head,
   nestled in the canopy.
A turn in the footpath, thick over-growth
   blocks the sun for a minute.
      Shadows, sounds, smells—
         transport me back to 900 A.D.

A shiver pierces my soul.
Decked in colorful dress, Mayans step out
   of the past,
      brush against me.
         The hair on my arm stands up
            with that soft touch.
I stare at crumbled ruins—crumbled times—
   straining to see with my eyes their faces
      and hear with my ears their voices.

The bees buzz in the tops of the trees.
   Where am I?
   When?
   With whom?
A step back in time, yet caught in between!
      Is it 1985 or 900 A.D.?
         or somewhere in between?

Had I been here before?
   At this spot,
   centuries before,
      standing at the foot of this temple,
         surrounded by my fellow Mayans,

         worshipping the god "Chac" and
            listening to the familiar

squeaks of birds
   and the laughter
      of howling monkeys.

The smell of incense fills the air—the mingled
  odor of honey and grain
    my sacrifice to my god.
The drums beat, beat, beat a familiar
  steady cadence,
     draws me to it,
      echoing my own heartbeat,
      and calls me to it.
The priests chat, chat, chat soft sounds
  that join the
    bass beat of the drums.
      The Mayan language a mystery to me
       yet I know its deep meaning.
I sway to the beat, the chat.
  It vibrates in my soul, calling me forth
    through the ages,
      crashes past time's barrier!

Dark bronze skin glistens in the firelight.
  Brown eyes search our faces for safety.
    Flat foreheads surprise me
      with their symmetry.
  I marvel at the feathery head dresses
    with multiple colorful gowns.
      I join the celebration,
        the ceremony!

Small, sturdy people crowd around me,
  greet me in a soft, rhythmic tongue.

    Gently, friendly—a spark shines
        in their eyes with recognition!
    We stand eye-to-eye!

THEY KNOW ME! I'm among my own.
    I'm home!!!

I rejoice in our reunion. My light skin shines
    in contrast to my bronze-skin brothers
    and sisters.
How can I explain our connection?
    We are centuries apart,
    tribes apart,
        languages apart.
Yet, here I am,
    at home
    and satisfied
        like never before.

I marvel at the ceremony,
    the rhythm
    the music
        the smells
            the community.

I have never felt more
    at peace with myself
        and my world.

But it can't be!
        I grew up in Colorado.
            Not Mexico
            Not years ago

Not Mayan

"Did you hear that? What was that?"
   my friend grabs my arm.

TRANSPORTED BACK
   GONE
      REALITY, or is it?
I'm back. 1985.

The jungle's summer heat presses in,
   the sun's scorching heat.
     Eerie sounds and hums flow
        through the air.
           Eerie, yet familiar.

I strain to hear it better
   to hear the beat of the past,
      to see those familiar eyes.

I want to return!
   But can I?

A MODERN-DAY PILGRIMAGE TO CHIMAYÓ

April 20, 1991

A modern-day pilgrimage to a
very holy New Mexico spot for Good Friday—
   El Santuario de Chimayó!

I drove a car; others did, too!
I worried I'd be the only one not walking.
I drove 180 miles from Raton, New Mexico—
   anticipating, wondering
      about how absurd this waste of a day was
         yet compelled to go.

Traditional pilgrims—walking miles
   sore feet and backs,
      walking sticks!
         Sweat, blisters, and dedication.

I studied the faces as I passed;

later, as I stood in line with them—
old wrinkle faces who had done this
    many times before,
the young being introduced to
    a lifelong tradition,
families—sharing a meaningful experience,
    an event mixed with the air of reverence
        and the joy of a picnic,
            mostly Hispanics, solemn.
Cowboys, hats, horses—hopeful,
    shorts, backpacks—water bottles,
Anglos—capturing a borrowed tradition.
    Dogs on leashes. An expectant atmosphere.
National Guard men caring our two flags—
    blowing in the cool mountain breeze,
        United States—red, white, and blue
        New Mexico—red and gold
            waving softly.

After driving 173 miles,
    anticipation mounted.
Finally, I first saw pilgrims
    at the east edge of Santa Fe—
a sprinkle. A few deserted vehicles parked
    along the roadside.
The farther west I drove,
    the more pilgrims there were.
        Steadily, the number increased,
            the closer we got to Chimayó.

Clouds hung low,
    threatening snow on this spring day.
We arrived;

    although I was alone in my car
        with Windy, my ten-pound poodle.
    I felt a part—a piece of
        something so holy and special—
    a part of a deep, reverent belief
        in a beautiful celebration.

Finding a spot, I parked, pulling off
    of the main road.
        I followed the hordes of people;
            I followed the sounds.
A priest spoke the words of the day on a PA
    system that could be heard from a distance.
I dropped down the hillside on a worn path
    into the sleepy village and

El Santuario De Chimayó.

Thousands of people–milling around,
    some in line waiting to enter,
    eating spicy burritos.
Some accomplished their task
    and enjoyed the leisure time afterward.

Large, wet snowflakes drifted down lazily,
    a New Mexico mountain spring gift.

I stood in line–silent, hopeful, drinking it all in,
    anticipating the event I had
        driven three hours for, yet wondering.
The Spanish language caught my ear—

the rhythmic voicing of words,
    so beautiful!

First, we passed through an old wooden gate,
    worn and sacred,
        touched by hands that came seeking,
            old, dilapidated, and marked
                with weather and time.
                      No rush, no hurry, no worry!

I touched it.
    I touched life and pain and times before me.
Other hands had touched it.
    Thousands of hurting, hopeful people ready
        for the blessings this place had.

Step by step, we meandered our way
    into the courtyard, a cemetery.
They buried people here in this place,
    special and honored.
Trees shaded this place–peaceful and serene.

We neared the door to the sanctuary,
    closer and closer.
        Massive wooden doors guarded
            this mountain treasure.

Finally, I entered.
    The dirt floor inside the door slanted
        downward.
A charged energy—anticipation—
        filled the air—
            solemnity of the moment.

No voices, only a holy silence.
   Incense, chili, burning cedar—
      luscious smells mixed
         with our anticipation.
People expectant of something—
   possibly a miracle.

Wooden carvings lined the walls of the church.
   Faded, colorful pictures—
      powerful meaning to those familiar,
         sacred stories told.

Shoulder to shoulder, two lines threaded
   towards the altar.
      People sat in the pews
         praying,
            absorbing the spirit of the place.

As we approached the altar, first,
   something appeared
      as diamonds lying there,
         sparkling and shine.
Then I realized—bags of dirt,
   holy dirt
      healing dirt.
         Why I came!

Finally, the altar rail—
   I'm there!

As I touched the bag that was mine,
   I felt it, the power.
On the altar, a bulto[1] stood, El Señor Santiago,

riding his horse, sacred.

We slowly threaded our way
   into a small side room.
      Oh, be careful—low door.
Then, another small room to the side.

The source of this holy soil,
   the hole in the ground.
I knelt down and touched it,
   prayed with it in my hand,
     rubbed it in my fingers,
wondering what I could do
   to commemorate this moment—
     pray, sing, dance, or scream for joy?
No, out of the place—not appropriate.
   Silence filled the room,
     the church.

Upon leaving, I passed through a room,
   lined ceiling to floor with evidence—
     thankful letters, abandoned crutches,
       and braces!
        So many pieces of
         evidence of healings—
          miracles!

I left the church; I walked around the grounds,
   shaded with tall cottonwood trees,
     almost in a daze.

Light, puffy clouds still filled the blue sky.
I felt so peaceful,
   connected,
   grounded to the Earth.
My hands still dirty and moist.
Alone, no one knew my name—
   yet a part of something,
      larger than me!

I wanted to stay!
   To drink in the peaceful liqueur,
   to watch more and soak it all in,
      but the snow returned.

Reluctantly, I left—to go north home.
Windy slept peacefully in the passenger seat
   but happy for my return.

The mystery of this age-old tradition filled me.
   My healing came with a connection with
      like-minded people
         a sacred place
            and my God!

A day taken from my busy schedule.
   A step back in time
   A day spent alone—yet apart,
     reflecting—
        listening from my heart—
           and fulfilling a dream—

**Good Friday at
The Santuario de Chimayó**

MY LOVE POEM TO MIKE,

My Wedding Day Poem to Misha

June 20, 1992

It is possible! Such a positive message was given
    to me, one and a half years ago.
        By me, by my higher power—
            who knows? I'm not sure!
It didn't include your name, your height,
    and weight,
        but it was you.
            Today, I'm sure of that.

Brought together in Albuquerque.
    A country girl just moved here,
    A Florida boy who found healing and health
        here.
    What brought us together to the special
        moment of commitment
            on June 20 at 1:30 PM?
    This date, Mike and I arranged.

The time was suggested by my dad,
    remembering my grandmother's
    superstition about getting married
    when the hands of the clock were
    going up; therefore, 1:30, not 1:00.
        Good luck to the newlyweds!
The circumstances of our meeting,
    neither of us controlled.
God's divine hand arranged the specific details.
    Common ground—interests, loves,
        needs, passions.

"Are you going to nurture this relationship?"
    he was asked by a loving friend.

Can we? Is it possible?

    Early on, I knew I loved Mike;
        I needed Mike;
        I wanted him!

But are we individually doomed—
    to sabotage a good thing?
        to abandonment?
            to aloneness?
                FOR LIFE!

What brought us to this moment of marriage?
    Mike's desire to do the honorable thing,
        grounded in a lifelong commitment.
    My desire to be with Mike
        in a permanent way.

Today, on June 20,
   I commit to you, Mike, my dear,
      to nurture our relationship,
         our lives,
            our lives!
I commit to run towards you,
   not away from you
      FOREVER!

Jealously, I will protect us—
   from the stalking enemy—
      the destroyer of happiness
         and the good,
            recognizing well
               it just might be us!

I love you, Mike.
   You're my precious gift from God.
      It is possible!
         Today, I know that and celebrate it.
   And I want to spend the rest of my days—
      in the shadow of your strong arms—
         and circled around me and my heart—
      next to you, committed to our
         common goal in life—
   close to you,
      because that's home to me!

WELCOME HOME, MISHA!
   WELCOME HOME, LARADA!
      IT IS POSSIBLE!

DAD

Harold Horner, my dad

1990s

Your stately frame
   like a windmill stood
    omnipresent in my life
      and childhood.
The wind of time battered and beat

your tall frame,
    only to make you more
        productive and vital.
The sounds of your workings
    clamored loudly in my life,
and oil was needed often to
    keep you runnin'—
the oil of understanding &
    Love.

HIGH HEELS

1990s

I gave up high heels years ago—
   I love their look
      perky & sexy,
      grown-up!

I had dreamed a little girl's dream
   to wear them
      in the grown-up world,
      not in play.

So, I did—
   for years!
Much of the time
   I still felt like
      the little girl dressing up,
         though!

I gave them up—
    practicality
        pain
            comfort!

The little girl misses the moments
    they produced!

SAILS DANCE

1990s

Sails dance across the
   silvery water.
Lilac smells caress the soft
   spot in my heart.
The bridge between my
   heart and head closed today.
I drink from the well of wisdom
   and fly high
   above the clouds.
Pain oozes out of my pores.
     And I shudder as I'm
     caught as a receiver of
        words.
I try not to conceal it
   from you, as I seek the
      depth of love.

Your eyes shine with love
    and pluck the pain
        from me!

SLENDER LIPS

Mattie Jesse Horner, My great grandmother

1990s

Slender lips
   that mirror hers.
I am her,
   Great grandmother Jesse.

Linked to my dad's dad,
    as mother and granddaughter,
Linked through the years by spirit.

Her frame pictures me
    because I am her.
Familiar eyes stare at me—
    mine
Slender, identical lips—
identical pain?

Deceived by love
    lonely by nature.
I never met her,
    but she is me.

As my life unfolds,
    will it be dark?
    will my lips be pursed?
    will death capture me?
        through painful adversity?

Does her spirit rule me—
    Am I really her?

YEARS & SILENCE

1990s

She looked over his shoulder
   lost in their silence,
     seeking conversation with
        what her eyes saw—
           over his right shoulder.

He sat, head bowed
   eyes down,
     looking at his food
       then the floor to the left of her
     but never at her.

They both ate toast and drank
   coffee—a morning ritual,
   simultaneously layering
     jelly on their toast—
something done for years!

Yet no words, no need to break
   the silence morning offered.

There was no hostility between
   them,
      only silence and years!

Now, a word,
   a nod!

Simple conversation and sharing!

A PART OF ME DIED

November 8, 1994

Hollow—that's the only way I can describe it
    HOLLOW—AND EMPTY!!!!

I know that a part of me died
    sometime
        somewhere
            for some reason.

It scares me.

A NEW MEXICO DESERT BREEZE

May 31, 1995

A warm summer breeze softly kisses my skin—
   no relief from the heat of the desert.
      Warm breeze that burns and bothers me.

Not like a cool Colorado mountain breeze
   or high New Mexico mountain breeze
      that refreshes and
         cools in bright sunshine.

Warm breeze blowing—
   defines the word "sultry."

A trickle of sweat down my back,
   a bead on my forehead,
      then another one!

The warm breeze doesn't cool or comfort.

It nags,
   teases,
      urges my body—TO SWEAT!

To cool myself down,
  to refresh myself,
    to relieve me!

My body can do that!

Warm breeze—no relief.

I LIKE IT!

Chapter Two
RIO GRANDE WRITING PROJECT, 1995

I wrote the following poetry during that inspiring time I took part in the Advanced Rio Grande Writing Project. As a part of this workshop, a local bookstore owner invited us to come and read our poetry at his bookstore—what a thrilling night that was! I read "Childless" and "My Bracelet."

At a Writing Project members' retreat in the mountains by Española, New Mexico, I took a walk through the woods, and nature screamed at me, so I wrote!

FORTY MAKES A DIFFERENCE

May, 1995

Is 40 a number or a milestone?
At 40, I was hurt, shattered, fragile,
   looking deeply at my life
      and what I'd lost
         or never had.

Is it a number? Does it signify anything?
No child had burst forth from my womb
   or sucked at my breast.
      Did this make me a success or a failure?

I remember the dreams of a 20-year-old—
   home,
      family,
         success,
            measured by how many
               children I had!

Did the lack of these signify anything?

40 and wondering—
  Is this all there is?
  Did I miss something along the way?
  Does this world make sense?
    Have I done anything of value?

Who am I?

I'm 41,
  and my perspective has changed!
There is a part of me that has died,
  but a greater part lives
    and lives with knowledge and
      wisdom!!

Forty is an important number,
  because I lived through it!
Because I have more awareness today—
Because I am willing to work hard on myself
  today—
    and
      because I've been given a sense
        of what is important

        —ME!!!!

CHILDLESS

June 30, 1995

The pain of being without a child!
   Eternally alone!
Empty cavity deep inside,
   waiting to be filled with life.
      Waiting, waiting, waiting!

I have no child to pass my stories on to
     my history, our history,
   how Grandad created our ranch,
   how special Branson Christmas trees are
     because we cut them down
       from our ranch,
        our land,
   how to do the jessie polka and waltz,
   how I was almost named Jesse.

My name, Larada, that should be passed on
   to my granddaughter,
      like my grandmother passed it on to me,
         every other generation
           for seven generations.

Cheated, robbed, failed!

Not woman, not mom, nothing!
   Does a child define a woman?
      Does the lack of them define me?

A miscarriage at twenty broke my heart.

Names and faces dance in circles in my mind—
   Lael Marie
     Marie for my mom
   Patrick Lawrence
     Patrick for Dave's dad
     Lawrence for my dad
Curly blond hair, blue inquisitive eyes.
Bright red hair, changeable hazel eyes.
   A mixture of him and me.
That miscarriage robbed me!

I have no daughter that has my smile
   nor a son with my dad's red hair.
No one to call me "Mommy."

The empty cavity waiting to be filled
   has grown larger
      no longer just my womb,
         but now my whole being,

    my every thought,
       ME!

Aching, lonely,
    pulsating to the beat of life
        missing what never was!

MY BRACELET

June 27, 1995

A birthday gift from writer/friends—
   a bracelet
      silver and dainty.

A constant symbol of what I've learned
   here being with you—
the circle I need to travel,
   not alone,
but with friends,
   writer/friends.

I must write by myself
   find the ritual that is me.
But I need you,
   your feedback,
   your listening ears and heart.
You complete my circle.

I will wear this forever
   to remember the brand
      you gave me,
         the brand
           we share—

WRITER!

ALONG THE WAY, NATURE SCREAMS AT ME!

May 30, 1995

Along the way, nature screams at me,
   "Look and see me here."
An orange and black butterfly
   dances in a circle,
     sucking sweet nectar and life.

A red rock half-buried
   screeches at me to see
     its bright color,
        its lasting character.

A woodpecker works hard
   at life.

A pine cone lays dry and brittle,
   once the hope of a new life.

A stick, simple
   dry and cracked
      wants to be noticed—
         to be touched and admired.

A bone—life given up—
   echoes a life lived,
      dry and bleached.

A coyote killed a raccoon,
   cleaned it of meat and
      sustenance.

Artifacts, pieces of life
   things here in the woods might have
      no value,
         might be trash to some people,
   but to me,
      life as it is—
         colorful, dry, and lifeless at
         times, yet teeming with life.

Tall trees bow to the earth,
   the weight of their existence
      dragging them down,
         the pain,
         the misery,
   closer and closer to the earth,
      Mother Earth,
         who nurtures and gives back
            life.

I see a stance of prayer
    of renewal, commitment
    yet deadly—pulling
        the life out of them—
    pulling, dragging, relentlessly,
        a cycle of life
            and death
        strength and overkill
            too much,
            much like life.

The sunlight shines brightly
    through the trees,
    but it's the shadows that call me.
A long profile of trees melts into one
    and shadows take over—
        dim, dark, cool,
    blackening the view.

Like feet, the roots of a tree grow down—
    supporting and balancing its
        tall counterpart.

Sounds abound.
    The quiet, gentle breeze whispers,
        "come see, come hear, come listen."

A pesky fly bothers me—
    my elbow, my thigh,
    my wrist, my ear,
    my hair, my everything—

buzzing, circling,
   demanding then gone.

The sun peeks through the top of the trees.
   Just a minute ago, shining full force
      on me.

Now, only a hint—like a light slowly
   going out.

A mosquito bite on my hip itches,
   demanding attention and care.

Bird racket echoes in the quiet.
   Someone's not happy.
   She demands her way.
      Her children are late in coming home,
   and she wants her male partner to form
      a search crew. He refuses to listen, so
      she continues to caw.

Wind sways the tops of the trees
   in a gentle rhythm to and fro—
   like a soft hand moving
      through the branches.
The sound is gentle yet strong.
   An unknown power moves them
   but only the tops.

A pine cone, rock, bone, tree
   connect me to life and earth.
   All a product of—
      laying there, ready to be seen.

Energized with power and strength.
Self-confident and knowing who I am—
   no questions,
   no doubt.
Strength connected to my Creator
   and creation.

The busy, insane life I left
   melts into peace and serenity.
I want to be a tree,
   standing firm in a forest,
      serenaded by the birds, bees, insects,
         the rocks and leaves.

The serenade of the forest,
   a tune that ears can't hear
      easily.
   Yes, you can hear the birds,
   but what about the trees,
      the dirt,
      the grass,
      the leaves.
A sweet melody of love,
   dependence,
   self-worth,
   assurance.

A jazz beat, a snappy samba,
      a slow, luxurious waltz.
   All these sounds unite in nature
      and play if you're listening,

    but not with your ears,
       with your heart!

The smells touch me—
    fresh and clean and green.
  Not artificial, contrived,
    but powerful,
      new,
        exciting!

Life-giving
  Alive
  Renewed
  A sharp contrast.
Deep meaning—

This is peace—
  this is serenity!
   Void of structure
    calm
      letting my heart listen,
        receive the message
        and alter my negative energy!

I feel it.
  I'm being altered
   right now,
     At this moment.

The lump in my throat is gone,
  that anxious twitch in my stomach

that dry, cotton mouth
the urge to run and do something—
   gone!!

Nature heals,
   but I have to be here,
     outside
        away from cities,
          demands,
          chores!!

I have to leave those distractions behind!
   Then nature heals!!

Chapter Three
1995-1996 WRITING WITH MY STUDENTS

While teaching language arts and literature classes in Albuquerque, New Mexico, I wrote daily with my students to begin our classes. During these two years, I focused on my dad's death, school life, and my life. Here's a sample of those writing times together.

I wrote on the same topic in two classes—look at the similarities of the poems and the differences!

PLAYING WITH WORDS

December 8, 1995

Catch a word
  and drag it by the leg—
    hold on tight.
      Don't let go!
      Hold on!
        Don't let it bite you—
        you might die from its
        poisonous bite or
          worse—

YOU MIGHT WANT TO WRITE MORE!

IF THE WORLD COULD HOLD US!

December 13, 1995
1st period

If the world could hold us,
    I'd be by your side every minute
        of every day.

I'd sleep with you, wake with you,
    dance with you, laugh with you
        daily.

If the world could hold us,
    I'd be in your arms
        and you, in mine, always.

I'd walk dusty mountain paths,
    marvel at the beach scenes and a lighthouse;
        twirl and spin in rhythm to a good
            country beat!

But I can't.
   What we have covers thousands of miles,
      years of commitment,
         a few short months together.

What we have sizzles and pops
   ignites in powerful explosions
      gently comforts and nurtures.

The world can't hold us,

   But I can hold us;
      you can hold us;
         we can hold us!
And that's enough this minute, today!

But—
   WOW—
   if the world could hold us!

IF THE WORLD COULD HOLD US!

December 13, 1996
3rd Period

If the world could hold us,
    cupped in its warm embrace,
        we'd be safe and secure
            to love each other.

We'd dance as often as possible.
    and vary the rhythm:
        waltz, cha-cha, and two steps.

We'd walk stormy beaches.
    and marvel at the
        power and majesty of a lonely
            lighthouse.

A lighthouse, sitting high up on the cliff
    because its job is to protect,

to warn.

We'd stroll on mountain paths,
    dusty, dry, and rich in color.

We'd hear the music of nature
    sings anytime we are there
        outside
        and together.

We'd hold each other tightly.
    in an embrace that would
        last a lifetime.

Wishes, dreams, possibilities?

Sometimes, I feel what we have
    is too big,
        too powerful,
        too mighty.

It's a gift
    from God
        good and pure
            but scary.
        enticing,
            sensual.

Does that doom it?
    Can it survive?
        Will it?

The choice of yours, mine, ours!

IT CAN ALL BE ALL RIGHT

January 4, 1996
3rd Period

It can ALL be ALL RIGHT.
    It can ALL be bad.

My perspective decides a lot of that—
    how I view things!
It changes like my underwear.
    I wish I were more consistent,
        but I'm not!
I'm moody.
    Controlled by the moon and the stars,
        the planets in their courses.
It's all very mystical.
    I wish I were more consistent,
        but I'm not!

I explode,

rage pulsating out of my every pore.
The world's my adversary.
   I wrestle.
      I fight!
         I complain!
           I skyrocket into emotional insanity.

The after-shock
   like a hangover—
      brutal,
         the taste of metal in my mouth,
           headaches
              pounding with too much,
                the endorphins scooting
                   around too much.

I wish I were more consistent,
   but I'm not.
I pulsate with pain.
   Energy buzzes through my body.
      No chance to sleep,
         only feel and feel
           and feel.

Chapter Four
1996 MY DAD

In my book, *A Time to Grow Up: A Daughter's Grief Memoir*, which I published in 2017, I said I wrote no poetry when Dad died. In preparing for this book, I looked through many journals and found these two poems I wrote about the fabulous storyteller he was and my heartache in losing him.

MY HUMOR

1996

My humor is awakened by
  the gleam in his eyes.
  Silliness that leaps from
    my little girl's heart.
  A contagious laugh that
    knows no bars.

My spirit is made strong by
  my past pain reconciled,
  living one more day sober,
  facing the illusions I've
    built, then accepting
      their dissolving right before my eyes.

Living without Dad,
  taking good care of myself.

A STORYTELLER FOREVER

My dad died January 6, 1996, and I turned to poetry to grieve my loss, remembering this moment.

May 30, 1996

Desperate eyes dart back and forth,
   looking for the words,
   the completion of a well-known story.
      Where did they go?
      They used to come so easily.

A stutter,
   eyes look down in frustration
      and despair,
   searching in his lap for the words—
      maybe that's where they went.
   Are they hiding in the folds of the blanket
      laying across his bony legs?
   He now clutches that worn afghan

with a death grip in his left hand,
looking for those lost words.

"I know his name as good as mine, but..."
   A plea to me to help—
     what was that name?
   Now, he looks to me for
     the missing words
       to you—
        to whoever still listens.

Hands wring in front of him
   again, the disbelieving wave
     across his pale lined face
       doesn't match, doesn't fit.

In the past, a master storyteller
   the words rolled off his lips
     timing and gestures
     added emphasis at the right place.

Smooth, humorous, total enjoyment—
   for him and the listener—
     often retold
     priceless
     well-known stories
Words, thoughts
   coherent connections
     that so easily came
       and came.

Today, total frustration—
   a struggle

    wordless moments,
        hours,
        days drag on for him
    because they don't come easy anymore.

It's easier to sit quietly
    than to struggle with the words,
        those damn words
            that don't come.
Time has robbed him—
    of the words,
        the connections,
            the familiar names.

But he tries again—
    eyes darting
        grasping for the
            familiar tale, the words,
    and I turn away
        tears streaming,
        sad and broken-hearted for the storyteller
            because he still has
                stories to tell.

It's not Alzheimer's
    or some deadly disease
        to blame.
It's age—
    years of life spent—stories told,
        old age,
    and it's robbed him here at
        the end of the very item that
        connected him to others—

    that he did so well—

    that gave him life—

      his stories!!!

Listeners—family and friends,
  where are you?
  Don't run away?

Chapter Five
1997

In 1996 and 1997, I was one of four teachers who represented Rio Grande Writing Project at the National Writing Project workshop, named Project Outreach Network (PON) in Princeton, New Jersey. Inspired by the outstanding teachers present and the rich learning environment, I wrote a poem about a dream I had about George Strait, my country and western hero.

WAS IT A DREAM?

1997 – Princeton University
National Writing Project - PON

It was so real!

Today, I still wonder.
It was a dream,
    or was it?

I was at the old Branson, Colorado gym
    at a dance
       like so many times before.
Sawdust on the floor
Country-western music
Familiar, yet so different!

The dance floor emptied.
I watched from afar—across the empty space.
    A new energy hung in the air.

Did everyone feel it? Did everyone know?

I had won my dream!
I won a dance with George Strait, my hero!
It only cost me $2—
   my dream.
     The ticket only cost me $2!
I couldn't believe it!

I looked at the dance floor,
   empty and ready.
A single spotlight illuminated
   our place.

George removed his black cowboy hat,
   grabbed my hand,
     led me to the center of the floor.
     The only couple there.
The music softly played.
   I can't tell you the name of the song.
     It didn't matter.

He took me into his arms,
   and the dance started.
My heart pounded as his body
   drew next to mine!
All I could do was look over
   his right shoulder.

In his quiet, gentle manner and Texas drawl,
   he spoke words that changed my life,
"Larada, you've got to make life happen.
It doesn't just happen. You've got to make it

happen!"

Our eyes locked, and I knew he held a
   deep truth for me.

We danced the two stepped
   in harmony—
      two dancers, one movement!

I finished the dance, snuggled close in his arms;
the crowd applauded;
and I woke up.

It was a dream,
   or was it?

No matter because its message speaks
   to me to this day.

No longer do I hear those voices
   that haunted me all of my life,
   those childhood accusations,
"Shit Kicker" when I went to Trinidad.

No longer do I want to hide
    my country heritage
      that told me Wranglers were
        the only jeans to wear
      and
      they had to drag the ground to be
        the right length.

No longer do I have to cringe when

>   questioned about my childhood and
>   I always felt less than—
>   just a simple country girl!

George showed me the deep truth
>   about my life—
>   it's okay; the path that brought me here
>   this day
>   may be different,
>   different from yours!

Mine was
>   a dusty country road
>   through the dry, hot plains
>   that mesas circle and crown
>   rattlesnakes buzz in the cactus
>   and
>   glorious sunsets fill the western sky.

I took the time to share this with
>   George Strait once—
>   a short note,
>   so, he knows!

I truly can make life happen today—
>   George Strait said so!

Chapter Six
1998

During the summer of 1998, my ex-husband and I traveled to Canada and the northwestern part of the United States. I played with poems, vignettes, trying to capture what I saw even if those moments were not mine but strangers!

CANADA

June, 1998

Mountains capped with glaciers
Turquoise blue water
   Rivers and lakes
Rock flows make them milky green.

Tall, skinny trees
   Firs and pines
German heritage
Campgrounds
   Showers
"Does the shower take a loonie?"

New phrases
   Kilometers versus miles
Canadian money
   Funny money
   Exchange

The rain came!

Search for wildlife
    Moose clumping in the riverbed
    Big brown bear beside the road
      in the rain
          turning over rocks gingerly
            looking for ants.
               Brown ears and eyes
               turned around
                  eating grass

River winding
Clouds hanging low on the mountains
    like cotton candy
Vibrant green grass,
    a color so different from the Southwest
        trees
Excessive water

Maps
    Places to go
    Places we went

Sleepy mornings
    Nightly rituals

Cool, not cold
    Heater kicks on—
        thermostat

Miles passed by;
    days do, too!

Words in silence shared.
   Laughter, too.

Safety created
   Words spill out on the page
      of days spent,
      of being.

Relaxation can help.
   I don't have to create it.
It settles in like a snug blanket.
It's a good book, a nap, silence enjoyed,
   words shared!
A deep sigh of relief
   of faith and God's goodness and myself.

LAKE COEUR D'ALENE, IDAHO

June 18, 1998

Lights on the shore.
   Blue magic reflects the lights.
Quiet except for a motor
   ripples in the blue velvet.
     A cool breeze wraps around me.

A LAUNDROMAT

Spokane, Washington
June 18, 1998

Ingenuity of children
Big Brother sees it as a race car.

Mom sees it as a laundry basket on wheels.
Little brother takes advantage of
   big brother's imagination.

Down one aisle
   Down another

Little brother's eyes glisten.
   Smiles and giggles filled his face.

For a moment, it was a race car—
   they raced

and won,
but mom interrupted the fun!
   "Boys, stop that!"

MY HEART WAS STRANGLED

>Spokane, Washington
>June 18, 1998

We finished a squared dance tip,
   and she came rushing,
      excited,
     glad to see my ex,
but his reception was stilted.

For one embarrassing moment,
the triangle that we were smothered
   me
        and her.

Finally, she squeaked out,
   "I just wanted to say hello."
But the moment was rich with electricity
   and my heart was strangled.

HE WANTED TO TOUCH HER

Spokane, Washington
June 18, 1998

He easily walked across the street,
   a few steps in front of her.
It was a gentle motion,
   not premeditated
      but natural.

He turned and held out his hand
   and she happily took it.
He wanted to touch her, feel her near;
   she wanted that, too!

A CHILD'S FIRST STEPS

Spokane, Washington
June 18, 1998

Timid, unlearned steps in the sand.
Dad, close at hand–
   not too close,
      but close enough.

He was adorned with a baseball cap
   and soiled pants
      but no shoes.

The feel of sand between his toes
   for the first time.
He wobbled and wove but kept going.

Mom videotaped the whole event—
   a chapter in his young life.

CONCLUSION

For the first fifteen years of my poetry writing, I played with it, just allowing the images and feelings to come forth. Topics varied. Free verse became my go-to when life handed me pleasure or pain.

I didn't realize it at first, but I was soothing my soul through words. The sleepless nights—the agony—the utter aloneness laid bare on the page! It was a kind of catharsis that I hadn't experienced before.

I had ups in life, and I had downs, as we all do, but I turned to poetry each time to capture the feeling, the nuance, the emotion, and in doing that, poetry healed my heart.

Poets think differently, see the world differently. I see possibility under a smooth gray stone, in the pathway of a dream, and in children playing at a laundromat.

I gasp at the creator's grandeur and grab a notebook. I weep over loss, mine and yours, and fit it in a verse. I focus on a topic like a photographer zooms in on a photo, to describe the details and what I see and what I don't see. Sometimes what I don't see becomes the mysterious topic from my soul!

The world is my canvas—my emotions drive me to look deeply at the subtlety others miss. And readers like you are so important to spreading my art.

I hope reading through this collection has made you realize a new love, or rekindled an old love, for poetry.

ABOUT THE AUTHOR

Larada Horner-Miller is a poet, author and essayist who lives with her husband in Tijeras, New Mexico—a town nestled in the east mountains above Albuquerque. She holds a bachelor's degree in English, a minor in Spanish, and a master of education degree in integrating technology into the classroom. For thirteen years, she was a beautician until transitioning into what would become a twenty-seven-year career in education.

She has written seven award-winning books and three cookbooks. She has also recorded three audiobooks.

Grab a free poetry book featuring my poetry from two poetry classes I took in 2002 and 2003 to sample more of my poetry here: subscribepage.io/VTpxUU

Interested in more information about Larada:
  www.laradasbooks.com
  larada@laradasbooks.com

ALSO BY LARADA HORNER-MILLER

- This Tumbleweed Landed: Life in the 50s & 60s in Rural America
- When Will Papa Get Home?
- Let Me Tell You a Story
- A Time to Grow Up: A Daughter's Grief Memoir
- Just Another Square Dance Caller: Authorized Biography of Marshall Flippo
- Coronavirus Reflections: Bitter or Better?
- Hair on Fire: A Heartwarming & Humorous Christmas Memoir
- Is My Truth Universal: A Woman's Poetic Journey - MY FREE POETRY CHAPBOOK

FUTURE PROJECTS & WOULD YOU...?

- A four-book poetry book series continues after-Book 1 - Was It a Dream?: Navigating Life's Journey Through Poetry
- A haiku poetry book
- How to write a biography—based on what I learned in writing the Marshall Flippo biography
- *An Eye Witness to Life* —a women's fiction
- And one more Tumbleweed book—more poems & stories about growing up in the Branson, Colorado area! There are so many!

AND NOW, WOULD YOU....?

I love this book because it celebrates the beginning of my poetry life. Each poem amazes me with its imagery and details.

If you liked this book, please go to laradasbooks.com to find links to the book and write a review and rate—that would really help me.

EXCERPT FROM BOOK #2 OF NAVIGATING LIFE'S JOURNEY THROUGH POETRY SERIES

I Dwell in Possibilities!

July 26, 2002

I dwell in possibilities...

It's a rich life
   full to the brim.
I face it in every question
   that comes.
I move from abundance.
I have all I need.
I have all I want.
   What a sweet refuge!

Life can come and go,
   but my worry is set at ease
      because of my attitude.

No one can crash through my armor,
    because I am safe and warm.

It's a life of plenty,
    of abundance.
I have no worries left.

My God supplies it all!

NOTES

A MODERN-DAY PILGRIMAGE TO CHIMAYÓ

1. Bulto - an image of a saint carved in wood and polychromed made in the southwestern U.S. and Latin America in the 18th and 19th centuries. https://www.merriam-webster.com/dictionary/bulto#:~:text=1,the%2018th%20and%2019th%20centuries

Made in the USA
Coppell, TX
19 November 2024

40402910R00075